There's a Box in the Garage You Can Beat with a Stick

Poems by
MICHAEL TEIG

AMERICAN POETS CONTINUUM SERIES, NO. 141

BOA EDITIONS, LTD. ❧ ROCHESTER, NY ☙ 2013

First Edition
13 14 15 16 7 6 5 4 3 2 1

For information about permission to reuse any material from this book please contact The
Permissions Company at www.permissionscompany.com or e-mail permdude@eclipse.net.

Publications by BOA Editions, Ltd.—a not-for-profit corporation
under section 501 (c) (3) of the United States Internal Revenue
Code—are made possible with funds from a variety of sources, in-
cluding public funds from the New York State Council on the Arts,
a state agency; the Literature Program of the National Endowment
for the Arts; the County of Monroe, NY; the Lannan Foundation for
support of the Lannan Translations Selection Series; the Mary S.
Mulligan Charitable Trust; the Rochester Area Community Founda-
tion; the Arts & Cultural Council for Greater Rochester; the Steeple-
Jack Fund; the Ames-Amzalak Memorial Trust in memory of Henry

ART WORKS.
arts.gov

State of the Arts

NYSCA

Ames, Semon Amzalak and Dan Amzalak; and contributions from many individuals na-
tionwide. See Colophon on page 96 for special individual acknowledgments.

Cover Design: Sandy Knight
Cover Art: Andy Hall
Interior Design and Composition: Richard Foerster
Manufacturing: McNaughton & Gunn
BOA Logo: Mirko

Library of Congress Cataloging-in-Publication Data

Teig, Michael.
[Poems. Selections]
There's a box in the garage you can beat with a stick : poems / by Michael
Teig. — First edition.
    pages ; cm
ISBN 978-1-938160-20-2 (pbk) -- ISBN 978-1-938160-21-9 (ebook)
I. Title.
PS3620.E436T47 2013
811'.6—dc23
                    2013013132

BOA Editions, Ltd.
250 North Goodman Street, Suite 306
Rochester, NY 14607
www.boaeditions.org
A. Poulin, Jr., Founder (1938–1996)

There's a Box in the Garage You Can Beat with a Stick

holy holy holy
there is no other story

wye oak

Me, I just lie around in the morning song of larks
and still make it over the abyss

Attila József

For Michelle

Contents

three

one

There is a day under a box

and in that day an engine,

and out from there a prairie
or a conversation amid kindness, between parking,
subject to all sorts of weather.

It is a Monday sometimes
though I know of no accord,

and it can be difficult; it can take
everyone you know, in a rainstorm
or an awkward sweater; it can be cold now.

Under one box are more shovels than
you've ever seen.

Under another box is a goose
on a riverbank slowly drifting away.

There is a woodblock and a stranger
or a series of strangers like side effects
you've never thought about.

It's very beautiful. There are delicatessens
and generations, and soon friends

and a little currency are sent in,
shoulders and grippers, and unstitching
there a road without appointment.

Under one box a man holds another smaller box
out in his hands like an invitation

or a detour you might duck into.
It's that kind of day.
It might last a lifetime or even now

a new conversation queues up the horizon
of alibis or model homes

a row of books the future
is always just browsing,
overlapping, leaving a person

or something like a person
in the dark without program.

There are friends who fade off
like movie credits
on the horizontal. How strange.

A woman you barely know holds
a grasshopper in her hand in a green dress

as if married or thinking of marriage
or simply recalling the marriage of her parents,
who were sweet people named after lakes.

There is a lot of going back and
going forth the sun's gadgets in thickets.

There were faces sometimes
and other times
the currents of a body

and you laminated among them
like a guest all the while.

A whole city stutters past
as they put it together, frame by frame,
inside of which are buildings or feelings,

or advertisements
for feelings.

The moon touches up windows.
The lights encourage campers.

Under one box are the offhanded flowers of our confusion
with their heads together like little explorers.

Some people send cards
and others reach out into the distance
like horses or causeways. Slowly,

haphazardly is how they do it,
one leg at one time.

Poultry Chronicle

My chicken has pointy ears
like a forest. He's long-thighed,

a non-sitter. That's him
in the low meadow then back again

at the porch door as if he's come
from a great distance and I have made tea.

He remains slightly tilted
and his keel low set.

Each night of their own accord
the stars drop down,

the coast drifts away and my chicken
drifts like a boat in a bowl.

In the dust he scrawls a whole cast
of houses and llamas,

a parade of broken soldiers,
a love letter to a strand

of women amidst streetcars.
It's the end of summer

and my chicken is on a boulevard
already filling with waiters.

He puts his ear to the ground,
his eyes close,

his mind like a wind instrument.
In it, there is time for everything.

Like a Satellite. Like a Stranger. Like a Waltz.

Onward I whispered and I passed as a man on a bicycle passes
in a suit in the evening, I passed meticulously,
my scarf in an upswing.

On the second try I passed a little wilted like a diary
and spat out a tinker toy into the dusk.
The moon lunged back.

I came by in a heap plying them with lilies and gum
and later gently like confetti
trailing down.

I came by on my own bike pulling another smaller bike
like a child by my left hand
which was tricky.

Onward I whispered to everything in its place: larch tree,
toll booth, satellite. My head pressed
against a lot of traveling.

I came around like a bunch of grapes but they would have none
and by the next time I was slushy,
the hole in my cheek humming.

The hinge in my neck bending, I saw my nose was the prow
of a boat, the night filling with fingerprints.
Onward, I whispered.

Right Now

There are canoes gliding the aisles of walmart,
wherein a pleasantness
can be motorized.

Wherein some new banjo
remains sunless.
Believed otherwise.

Wherein explorers
discover
the greatness of sparklers.

This horizon too fills
with a distant shiny music.
Disposable canaries,

the weather here is skittish.
Am I afraid of lunch?
A little.

And still a line stretches out
towards what must
be evening.

O everlasting thermos,
I am cold
and the sky

fills with bargains.
O indelible monitor,
fog clouds

the gardening sector
and when it lifts
it's an ordinary day all night.

Undid

It was noon when he awoke like a god
and put his ear to the wall
and realized it was an ear too.

He put his face to the weather
and could hear

the way a whale hears
through its throat.

He did not speak.

When he opened his eyes
birds came to measure the afternoon.

Clouds came and he went driving by himself
like a god might;

he went everywhere,
his head locked in that music.

He put his ear to the bank
and it was buzzing.
His ear reddened.

He put his ear
to the ground like a squirrel
and the world passed
over and through him.

Already there were dents in the river
and in the hill pitched with trees,

and in the strangers
reaching out like postcards.

There were dents in his friends
and one in his face
where the sound came to pool
for a bit like a news feed.

At night he could hear for miles;
he could in the dark grin
and the darkness would grin back.

For a moment a pinhole he bent his head to,
the night is a small future.

It lay open before him.

He put it on and for an hour

he was the field the moon
would not rise in.

He was the thistle,
the stump a redwing alights,
common as algae,
a lung in the ferns.

He took it off.

By then other gods moved about
like businessmen or institutions,

their names crammed with noise,
their voices minty.

On the nightstand an empty glass;
his mind on hiatus.

His mind a hotel people came to
and lost socks or made babies

or just sat there diligently
in front of the TV
feeling talented.

I hear you, he said.

On the wooden chair
a repetition, moments
becoming escalators.

The escalators becoming infrastructure.
The infrastructure already something
he almost knew washing over him
for as long as it takes.

He put his face to the lilac
and it was awful
sawing back and forth.

He held his wallet to his face
like a tattoo.

He moved through this place,
and the faces pressing
against his face

this vibration
or October again
and again a particular

and impossibly remote afternoon
banking off the sun

then spilling out everywhere
like a memory or a childhood.

The people shouting and the music.
The rivers and buildings.

The cars moving their petitions in circles
and in the distance
alphabets and winters.

The world was shiny.
He could hear water pouring
from the mouth of a machine,
objects broadcast across the surface of a day.

He put his ear
to the bread breathing
shallowly on the countertop.

His big idea took the garbage out.
His small one moved to the right
and slammed into a doorway.

I am writing this letter
he thought, for the last time,

though you are not here and I will not send it.

On the grass this morning
another score of crows.

I am making you this shirt, he continued,
one arm outstretched like a voice,

one summer
moving out into the dusk
where the sky gives off its prospects.

He put his face to the door.
I'll rest here, he thought,
until I figure out who does the talking.

A Little (more) About Me

I am self-unemployed.
I have another side of me also,
all wussy.

Catapults into the darkness,
I like to think,
grave as a stranger.

My dread of my father
is great. Also money
and advice.

Also hammers and mistakes.
That February when
you stopped calling,

and the trees moped around
like teenagers.
As the maker of the motion

I can speak
to the motion.
It's fucked.

Handcart to the parking lot,
I like to say,
ghost ship to the horizon.

I am right now one centimeter
from humming. OK.
I am humming.

if it's still called that

and the world around me was like
a drowsy clerk's office where one rheumy

intern made jokes and the other
kept interrupting my stories with stories

about his own childhood which was
far sadder than mine and had taken

a long time to reach us so full
of banquets, sirens and retractions

that we stopped to play cards for a time
by the service entrance with a view

and when he continued he spoke plainly
of several hundred years of pain, toolsheds

and drifting snow and the other intern,
a halfwit, and I huddled closer

and from the small bits of his story
we imagined the girlfriends and snowmen he once knew

and the moon lodged above a notebook
unable to breathe as a stranger

entered an emptying station
and cut his initials swiftly into a bench.

One Cadet Crashed

past the test-site scarring the hillside
the red barn blistered with vines
we run into stoplights and antennas

and the conversations we'd lived through and the places
they'd made in us then past the outbuildings and orderlies
where neon sentries bow out of sight

and we are alone finally on a faraway
road backlit by traffic
all of us shouting or crying and

some stopping to give speeches,
some whimpering and approximate
and diminished already like history

or the moon out here in its lab coat
attaching small characters to the fields
with glue, but bolts are used on the larger ones

and several of my friends wrap their arms
in a thick music and their heads begin to vibrate
and I must be rubbing my eyes

as a cluster of starlings rise up like a shudder
all of us blinking in each direction
in that new dark lit only by breathing

Where I Come From

They drink to your health how many
times you tire of counting,

to your afterglow, pilgrim, your cinders,
your infinite blinks unsalted.

One tomorrow an applause of poolballs;
one a sudden gap to mind.

The late fall fires bank into
the outreaches. It rains slogans.

It rains ducks. It's raining
strangers of the normal size.

Here's to the frogs
blistering the roadface.

A girl walks the street calling Samuel
and all the Samuels surrender.

In Their Numbers

The evening fashions a man at a pulley,
an armchair in front of an outlook,

unfenced sky, many cities, father
of some furniture. Thus screens.

One man pulls scenery up he almost
understands: Milk, cigarettes, lotto,

pokeweed, mooneye.
He rises into place the way

a name travels—an ordinary passage
poured into—chickens and bitters, zip codes,

pistols, some persons of interest,
some partial, some tickets

are turnips. He's Polish.
Some helpers not helping.

Evening passes out bears against weather,
this business of courage—the world

falls to pieces. Guesswork,
jumpsuit, he tips his head

back, sidelong, and holds
his son to one ear like a radio.

When I Said I'm Changing Hats I Meant It; This Hat Is Crummy.

It's a playground hat, the one
where the citizens turned on me
like a thicket. An execution.
This hat is no longer my policy.
It is impossible to fend off
even an ant with such a hat;
I congratulate the ants.

I am unfurling my incredible new hat.
It displeases the moon. It is without
prospects, which is why I like it.
It is a congenital yeti, my hat, a context
for the birds. Crowned with a garland
of such refuse, what god should I ask:
Who steals the feathers from my hat?

Like many great things, my head
is in it. My Hungarian boat.
My dearest beaver, we stopped to rest
at the holy fig, then sacked a city
with my hat. My matchsticks
on parade. My head smokes.
My hat is open for reception.

My speechwriter, whose own head
has just now been softened by a sneeze,
is there and his stepsister is orbiting
the tequila in my hat.
She comes around; I come around
(It's my hat). My rain-soaked cantina,
TV flashing, my tourists.

Once excited I will tell you anything
but then feel bad about it later.
My new hat keeps its own counsel.
The sunlight there is a success
the speechwriter's sister and I
can hardly contain.

Now inside of a man

an airplane
drifts in the overnight rain
off course

over the new couch,
greengrocer, eclipsing
warily the corner

where cranes assemble
a familiar
incoherent feeling.

There is an abundance
of pistols,
if you need a pistol.

Steady gossip,
pharmaceutical curtains,
there is to the right

an unexpected memory
into which Minneapolis
might fit,

inside of which
is a mixed drink he mixed.
Inside of one city

piece by piece another city
taking over, adding rabbits,
subtracting tantrums,

townspeople determining warehouses
and children, moviegoers,
don't give up—it's descriptive.

A punch of moonlight.
A sufficient aviary.
An absence in a landscape

where the shovels bank
and he leans
for a moment

feeling
for all the world
like Canada.

Have I Forgotten Anything

I go out like a slogan
in the morning. Everyone does.

The cat eats a butterfly.
The sun being prolific.

It's like a sequel.
The world moves

around in vans and I
man the mixer.

One dog barks then
the spaces between them are barking

and then a hummingbird like
a tiny green zipper opens the air.

It's a perfect day.
All the old people start mowing.

It's a nice day for a parade
and here comes one

moving slowly on the horizon
like an addendum.

two

under one box another box

I head off like an inventory
      like a kindergarten
under one box is a pie
      the sky too is a box
           into which
we turn to each other
      take stock

maybe the sky accidentally
      knocks over a box
so that a new person spills out
and gets included

They Did Not Come Close

Were they sleepy, sticky? Mistaken
for a chimney? What yawning is?
Are they assembled for such occasion?

What occasion? Whose memory and
in whose body so vast and painted,
partial walkways and verandas.

Who passes there sidelong naming
buildings or foothills? Likewise
fears? Weren't they life-size?

Did it hurt much? Did the strings
break? Are the trees wrong? How
torn? Why helping?

Whose eyes in what calm or
lightness or lining the courtyards like
currency (pitiful) and so what?

Who bargained? Whence dreaming
and, if by then animals and a litany
of circumstance or apology,

then some new moon to outstrip the
harbor, one account wedged
invariably against the next.

all of them nice people I think.

This one an affliction.
This an arboretum.

This one so naïve
he imagined himself

lit up from within
like a lantern or a mountain

on a barstool.
Some well-scrubbed

or suddenly comprehending
as if shot to film—

the small one who later died
from a hurt in his eye

received as a boy
from a stick

and this one's leg a bit longer
from dragging by a horse,

all of them hurrying along
like calendars

or mistakes, provocations,
for instance my beard,

if you recall, like something
tremendous attacking my face

and the air
just around it.

One More Time

A man walks out
each morning and gives

a glass of water to a rose
in its slab of sunshine

in his mind messengers
a few catchphrases since years

since villages since one supervisor
is not like another supervisor

this life is scratchy
he may step back with care

and still the landscape remains
a handful of lines

that cling to him as he moves
at this hour buying groceries

and elsewhere inventories
his true work patience

a slow rain of effusiveness
and organizational problems

so shut up he thinks
still wearing the little slap they gave him

on this channel weather
then the history of weather

then a butterfly
rises up to knock

a boy down in a backyard
his true work caution

two strangers touch shoulders
on a street corner

where the evening shifts
its crowds dissolve

together giving up a single
cup of coffee or puff of smoke

a clutch of birds drawing out over
the museum and a few ordinary

names or hours as he rises and circles
as he has been practicing

all these years
so that he might

rise and circle
one day a bit

more gracefully as if
nothing happened ever

Till It Sticks

They wooden hut. They walk backwards.
All of them helmet-wearers.
One may sit in front of the shut-down hotel
slicing his egg. He may infant,
struck dumb in the meadow.
He may phone into the distance
and the distance may phone back.
In this way thinking spans themselves.
Without an anthem they go out
of their heads, so their sidewalks
are soundtracks. It comes in bunches.
It pops in boxes.
Day and night they trouble.
Even the dolphins are for sale.
Swan in no box. Ten on the hippo.
Their market mooing.
Their arguments leaking. Into it
smugglers and hustlers snuffing
small dealings. Into it antlers.
Their weather unwilling. They splinter,
joined again in cupolas,
in minuets. They creakbed.
That is, they burble and
the darkness burbles back. Sometimes
sisters. Sometimes dumplings.
A litter of clappers and chatter.
They smolder, keep quiet,
then flock to tables in twos
till the trouble stops.
Their borders are breakable.
Everything burns,
not even close. They so long
so well they're already leaving.

Short History of Kites

Spring shows up with a costume of turtles.
Its ears full of newts. Its audience
of scientists.

At first we just eat it. The day a boat
we are dreaming and that boat
doing business.

Spring appoints hammerings:
the afternoon unsettling sun dresses
and on the street corner

for a moment one hat plying the air.
The first kites were also
the first movies—

cutouts against a collaborative sky
held by a line that pictures
a horse beginning

to lope or a dragon
rushing the sunrise, the morning
not wounded. Hand held.

Some people talk about life like a sandwich
or a bandage, someone's mule
eating an apple.

A boy is a body stretched everywhere.

I came here tremendous
in a suit of gunshots
how restlessly
in a hat of sleeplessness
otherwise humble.
Further north another
noise knelt beside me
another breathing
hard to understand
and the new rain
straddling cornstalks.
I came here incredulously
like one thought
approaching another
for the first time
visibly wary but
nodding along fiendishly.
Hello Friend. This
is my everyday sweater
my chinstrap rattling.
Never mind the sinkholes
I kept moving
at times sheepishly
others grinding my seasons
and scenes together
until I came here
of many minds,
above ground,
where it's April everywhere
so incredible
and smashing everyone
who looks at it.

When I Pass Out I See a Pleasant Vista Heated by Coal

friends come down carefully in the distance like
snipers and motor homes, much coveted, smelling
of tree trunks and paella, of casinos, they come
suddenly floating through the air dressed as
newsletters or collection agencies, a place to think
for a moment or in this light sometimes radios in
the middle of life urgent and flustered; they walk
backwards deciphering roll calls, solvency,
aloneness, and with them carry matchbooks
sweetly and frequencies or mustering courage they
make a kind of gap in life, thank goodness, not as
curtains or subways but as they have to, as
boulevards or families or perhaps constellations
however monstrous and insufficient and as I
remember it we kept our pants on generally longer
than one should, looking fine, we say, most of us,
and it's true, our pants are lovely.

My Little

Onward I whispered and my
cat seemed weary out among
the philosophers and busboys
on a side street of the evening
in that other incomplete city
where the moths rise up like
retorts from the shrubbery.

Homemade Whelping Box

I got a terrarium
with attached warming light

and this marvelous
label maker,

& a blue-plastic-
bowling lady

on the kitchen table
dwarfed by a lemon

in the darkening house.
Farewell torments,

I will take
your bagged leaves.

I will pick up your laundry
and make with it a fence

in the new backdrop
we can hike back and forth.

I got a worm farm and
this alphabet puzzle mat

and some items just for staging,
like a pillow that props up your back—

A husband. Two chairs
in front of morning and

this virtually-blue forest.
I'm looking for a snow coat,

no bells or whistles.
Me and my family
will come pick your apples.

The Gate Snaps Open

In the evening
something actually beautiful
chews at my ear.
That's you, Shrub Doctor,
our life together
growing bushy.
Hear that? That's
our lawn dying,
our neighbors
clobbering each other,
a cylinder drops
into the vacuum
at the bank and soon
we're broke again.
Let me help you
out of your overalls:
you can help me
off with my beard.

The sun is an example of what? A light burning over a donut.

The wooden handle
to the arbor opens
the topic of the sun
a tunnel. A toll.
Small tooth. Bright tangle.
A wind backs up
a litter of pigeons
who unbind like a book.
The sun splits the difference.
Have I got this correct?
The sun is a reading machine.
Something sweeps over
the hill, unmistakable
pixel, auditions the red barn's
red barn door
and settles behind us.
The sun shines champagne.

Oafish

I had a feeling of cease-fire,
my nose in the air like an air force,
my enemies forgetting me.
I had a broom in my teeth,
my butterfly open all morning.
From this position I couldn't say.
Time is a hunting dog.
Snow goes on.
I am a wedding guest.
I am flying out to meet you,
as far as mountains,
as far as dumplings,
as far as the dumpling mountains.

My other thought rides a bicycle into a tree.

Late at night my other thought
stands in a puddle in the kitchen
with a nimbus of fruit flies

and the fruit flies consider the legacy
of my other thought;
All fucked up, they conclude.

I make allowances and my
allowances make what are called
rotten decisions,

terrible choreography,
and when I step back
from that they've made martinis.

I unfurl my banner and my other
thought furls it. Is this repetitive?
I unfurl my banner.

Of course I saw the tree
fixed in the streetlight dimly.
It's still out there, magnanimous.

Too often what seems
like a good idea
later is a contraption

pedaling off with your time:
See my other thought
lodged in the arch of a bridge

on the banks of the Tiber.
It's antismoking
and I hope I'm smoking.

Seriously troubled it occurs to me.
A little pudgy, says my other thought.
Crows staff the high branches.

I consider retorts
while my other thought
settles down on the internet.

Do Pete and Jane
earn more than me?
Probably. They are super hot.

Self-Portrait: Swimming in Monkeys

A quiver of pines. A parcel of monkeys.
Any of several long-eared monkeys,
usually collating. Usually a stranger,
or several strangers at once.
A collating monkey. Probably a man.
For many years over many tables
a registry and other panels. Compare with coping.
A pressurized modular component. Web
monkey. See also chitinous—it's stupid.
A clump of boys unintentionally difficult.
A clump of toys. A cord. Probably simpler.
See fuzz. See blue candy wrapper.
A similar sentence. The apartment
at dusk is empty or picked
clean, the swallows passing
into the brambles unbidden.

Whereupon Lydia Sparrow

To not unhinge with the unhinging day
which pulls up in a yellow limousine

she half recalls or wants to,
and the roofs are part of it

slowly, or people's failings. She hears
the hammers but what are they building?

The days are long and incline together;
she heads out in a blue dress already

tired of such deposition—it's best
to leave and leave an absurd note behind,

something about the proportions
of heaven, feelings divining August,

its scaffolding a surplus of porches
and conversation where the vines break open.

Thank you for the glass, she notes.
Thank you for the water.

All at Once

boys on their bicycles
shout in their cell phones

a bit of correspondence
as loud as they can

everyone around here
pedaling or transparent

the moles inch down
many smallish autumns

one boy breaks from the rest
and smiles a little, nothing spectacular

one soldiers on, his plastic
feet forever molded together

through medication
or sunglasses

an assemblage of bottles
preface the porch stair

and I have forgotten
what I meant to say

when the horizon
again opens its kiosk

Optimal Brain Institute

In the pain-processing portion of my brain there is, at present, a
backlog; there is a short film playing of a man smoking a cigarette
under slightly rearranged stars whose main failure lies in the
inability to recognize certain patterns. In this part of my brain the
circuits seem broken, which could prove useful if you're involved
with the government or wrestling or if the damage produces a
thing that is not pain—perhaps it could produce popcorn or
girlfriends or something large and beautiful in the summertime like
an elephant or a stranger or many strangers if you could meet
them singly, say in a hotel room or along a promenade wearing an
effortless hat or following the water down the shore where in one
story swimmers start out untroubled into another glowing
afternoon, the weather OK even when there is no weather.

The Small Ones, in White

The world is so full now
this thought won't reach you,

my winter anthem,
bunny:

it is snowing. Fall
schedules its frequencies

letting go the brown bears,
new brides, small doubts.

Dumb turbine, the heart
too is a machine.

Sometimes a dirigible.
Sometimes a girl's choir.

Young Fly Catcher

Out here we're in the group called Odd Jobs.
We seize the fiddles; pound out the light.

It's morning and the boss says Cement.
We clean the sand; sell the starlings.

We surmount the hurdles one by one
on the flipside of my tie I write the questions:

Can I ask you a question?
Can you see the ocean?

I hear the man fidget on the phone's other end
and realize he's probably out in the yard

not looking for the cat, out
in Ohio, pockets full of kindling,

the phone at his head like an afterthought.
The ocean, he says, bores me senseless.

It OK, I tell him, I'm a bad salesman.
My headset is hurting me.

The clouds press down,
he lets me know.

We press the clouds down, I tell him.
We crack and test-hop; we go on air.

We free the zephyrs.
You free the zephyrs, he says.

Slow Motion Research

The mind settles down
among chair legs, piano scores.
The name tags I lost.
When it is called evening
I go out walking,
the sweet ones
in my pocket.

I Make Mistakes While Sleeping

I'm happy to hang out here,
where the side effects

slosh around, and let
my fingers trail

in the weather.
Dear heart,

it was late and
I was among you

and my errors
were everyday—all of them

making progress,
changing cities, growing lettuce.

They were raising
chickens, checking feed stores;

all of them flower
carriers, sleepy panelists

unfolding over weeks
or sometimes looking down

a shred of sunlight
memory puts out,

while all around
a rain of miles

staking out a future
more perfect or worthy.

How dim it seems or
acquiescent, how loud.

The crowds thin
into a difficult

show of hands
and as I remember

now is a good time—
a few thuds in the background

where the paint gets applied
and on the scaffolds

some men are making
things interesting.

The Flag Was a Kind of Flannel

In those days I was lived in—I couldn't help it. I had only one suit, which usually appeared holding a daisy as its arms filled with grief and small talk. It paid its respects and my respects and as such was more of a curtain than a flag. Behind it a battalion of moles readied the earth. In it a lining of caterpillars blue one minute and the next busy mending and in the next blinking into an event at the border between me and the world where the acoustics got blurry. That suit kept my act together, so I left it there and went out walking by the whirring of felt at National Felt. There was the nearby and a bruise that looked like a cloud, and against such weather my suit, which had gone up ahead, already clearing a low fence and not looking back.

three

Divisions of the Book

Book 1 of the heart, a note in a blimp made of tinfoil

Book 2 of the machines that make blimps & the concourses of air

Book 3 of conduits—the air rearranging itself to disclose breezeways
& the avenues gathering sneakers and front stoops, first ordinary
sparrow, porchlight

Book 4 is more like a swordfight than a marathon, more secretary
than astronaut, more explanation than stun gun, more snow of every
kind unconvincingly and on the cities of the world I have never seen
as if by mail

Book 5 of the retreat, which was, as they go, a formality. I set out at
dusk with a child on my arm and a cat off the path in the brush behind
us drifting and stars of course however loopy or crude

Book 6 of being filled by a valve every minute surrounded by wires I
swear it everything I say is true

Book 7 drunk enough

Book 8 I have put my head in the direction I was tilting and slept
there

I Start Over by Simply Loving the Cat

When they say my short-term memory impairment
makes it difficult to say
if my working memory is working
I say, This is my retinue of donkeys and anthems.
When they say the pain processing circuits of my brain
break down and thus produce more pain
and that pain is then amplified
by any new pain, pranks included,
I say, The soul's nearness.
The future makes things.
Because it has legs the future
makes things like high buildings and bodies
to be singled out or to be touching
or in a style that is touching.
A widow's poor memory might
leave her at the table some mornings,
a lovely blue still burning off and
outside a new small boy clasping
an orange in his hand like a planet.
To get out of your body can take half an hour and
I have seen friends broadcast
past a progression of couches.
I mean it is lovely in the garage.
The sun made us a place for reflection.
All birds are descriptions. All tools are true faith.
The sun made us—the minutes
skewing forward small fires turning slowly.
The sun not even liking us.
How to tell the others?

Hazard Avoidance Routine

One night grows letters,
one launches fathers.

One letter ends
with a rollcall of oceans:
Sea of Azov, Gulf of Lions.

One father grapples with the distance
and produces a shed in the tall grass.

The brain flings out mail.
By the shed a pond is poured
and from the opposite shore
the sun is a subscription.

Some fathers are fickle, some dented,
some double as a lullaby
or in the afternoon
a lump, uninterrupted,
a stick in his hand like a ticket.

He pulls up a chair,
the outlook a switchboard.

He hangs a door
and his attention hinges.

His letters rehearse a landscape
planted with portals and lampposts,
a diminutive bridge on which a shawl
in the farness waves
like a paint flake.

Those, he thinks, are flowers.
Those are blind men. Grandmas.
Those are chimneys. Grief.
Ice storms. Those are firemen.

He sits on the porch
and considers a bucket.
His mind is a farmhouse. A gray mouse.

Some letters are furious as if squalling.
Some fathers are meager or peachy,
among the birches and sticklers.

They perform calculations
like I'll be with you this minute.
I'm just resting my eyes.

your staff has misplaced my file

I kept my head low and those who claim
they saw me marching in the band

full of sleeping pills and glitter
were in some other parade.

I closed my eyes and awoke
in a cubicle not making a sound.

In my mind I'd made a parking lot in my chest
and paused there, like a barmaid, conscientiously.

I made a clearing where the shouting world piles up
dimly on the horizontal, as it always has.

A fog was filling the horizon with beauty queens and waiters,
with ghosts and platelets. With cellos. I'm sure of this.

There are other lives out here I'm having—
Other palaces, carriages, other catalogues.

Did I get locked in the storeroom? Many times,
and in the dark I dreamt of theme music:

A human thing, I swear it. Each horse
I rode in on rode out the same night.

Some Sleep Is a Rerun

Some sleep is a rerun,
a hiccup of days in hammocks,

of cracks in arches, of percussion,
or situation: a gnat in the nostril;

a cat at the portal;
a fold creases a stone.

Sometimes at sunset
a gunshot:

the world so serious
serious music gets piped in.

They call it genetic.
The lights go out, bridges raise

and a vast province
of storefronts and habits,

a pothole of feathers
or fathers,

a boy on a boat
in the difficult snow.

I rinsed my face and wished to be rid of it.

Also cell phone towers, sad endings,
dickheads, and the rich. This memory
and the one just now replacing it.
This recurring tomorrow.

Also certain types of facial hair,
authority, remaining calm, learning
about what you're missing.

This summer was one of various scenarios:
constant lawn mowing, recorded dance music,
useless and wounded negotiation like a diary.

Also addresses carried away.
Also they have their own minds.

When I learned what I inherited—
a poor navigational device—
I didn't like it. I loved it.

When I stepped back I saw my grandfather
lure a cow from a burning blue barn
and how little he said, our numbers decreasing.

Also how large our heads were,
how angry our village.

I saw the sky too
a habit we already miss.

I Abandoned My Plans. I Had No Plans.

Some men are so lazy
they should be revered as saints.

Not improved. Not working.
No lift or tilt.

Trying to put on one sock
in the morning they are one man.

A centipede of trouble.
He pretends

to be hit with a stick.
He looks at the world

as though it arrived in an airplane.
The new world's new, quickening sun

taps the stadium whose retractable roof
pulls back till a single crow comes out,

sideways, slurring over the skyline and wires.
It lays out evidence and empty space:

A woman beside you sleeping. A little clerk
hurrying past like all the capitals of Europe.

Drowsy projectionist, the sun
does nothing but ticket the leaves.

Some men are so beautiful that their insides
are lined with the skin of lions,

with the narrow skin of birds.
With no help from me,

the names of ships, with
the teeth of mice, the overdue snow.

I've Been Unwell & Now I'm Well

I've been unbuttoned
in the courtyards,

by the water's edge disheveled.
Already I've said too much.

Among the tender prospects
I was cold. A stranger.

I shut down and
awoke in the park

with the sun
flustered through treetops.

I opened my eyes
and a sogginess set in,

or a greatness,
a great sogginess.
I closed my eyes.

Night Jar

In a light rain
flowers light the highway

where everyone's motor
is already running.

The world is baroque:
my apartment is small.

America is monstrous.
The phone rings

in everyone's pocket,
but I remove my feet.

I'm finished.
For a long time

a rat in the wall,
a dog in a panic,

an abandoned season
by the sink to which

the moon makes
an excessive offer.

Yesterday's moth broke
down on the sill.

Yesterday's headlines
flattened like veterans.

One dumpster, four pigeons.
All manner of men.

Say Uncle

People still recognize me. They say, Oh,
you're that wrestler guy. You made
three mistakes. Your lips
are still moving. They say as big
as two boulders, a lifetime of mallets.
Quick, they say, grab my hand.
The world grows dark. No hitting.

For what transpires there is no excuse:
flying headscissors, broken shoelace,
barking mountain. To lie like this
on your back signals defeat.
Everything tastes like rubber.
Everything looks like clouds.
I put up my white flag.
Leap onto your knees, they say.
They can't get enough of that.

I Am Walking to You Now

Each morning for years
I sit at the desk like a treaty.
How bruising.

In one corner a type of whining
is heard and in the other
a diagram points out

all the things
that don't get done
or seem suspicious.

For example, this afternoon
was spectacular,
the first in a series

starting dimly
like an expedition,
and then what?

This afternoon
was perpendicular.
Might I suggest better snacks

or record keeping before
the initial enthusiasm
fades in a stampede of trifles?

No. I am texting you
my peanut. In addition
to rambling

I am in extraordinary cases
able to extricate myself
and stand for a second

born on the promise
of another
rust-colored morning.

Hello daylight.
You look deliberate.
I am money not in the bank.

I Got News for You

My rescue plan calls for chicken wings,
for patience wagons. Leopards and alligators,

I am running. These, my invitations, are
sleepless and woozy by noon.

Stop whispering. It's February
and they owe no explanation.

It's nighttime and
my head is sunny.

Between us stairs come down
and out of them

the most amazing contingencies.
All of them perfect. Some of them people,

some ponies steadfast
in a snow of sudden doubt.

Did I mention feathers? Robots?
My rescue plan calls for a recount.

Bulldozers and well-wishers,
I am married. A rented moon and its temporary

caucus, and, however disheveled,
I have the armful of daffodils.

I have the reassembled heart.
It hearts you.

In a Small Boy Blinking

The fur freezes on a moth's collar,
the deer lick at the field's end
where he scours the ground

and gathers the wood
then walks like a mechanic
around the afternoon.

The animals in it
that go unused
like once a heron

very green,
interrupted in silhouette—
a bird in a bracket,

not an example
of anything. On one side
a real horse.

Unchecked, the world has grown
grasses. There was a man feeding
the horse an apple

and a passing girl's
white dog passing and
in the next moment ghosts.

Into the afternoon
crowds of people covered
in functions or nearly

swallowed by boxes.
Towards evening
he's appointed to snow

and to snow all night
on the thin roads and
distant interiors

and the television
snowing in the sleep
of his mother.

He goes on thinking
the morning might be two factories:
one making felt

and the other sheet metal.
One making bluebirds
and the other subordinates.

How many coats cascading,
briefcases speckling?
How many mothers?

His receptor's sputtering.
A touch could be counted.
Another valve opens his mouth

and to the east the sun
is rolled in like a monitor
by a janitor,

trees swabbing the sky.
The gears must be
very tiny. Not tethered to sleep

he comes down
to breakfast.
His father's a forest.

He pulls on his clothing.
His father's at work.
It's Monday.

His father's downstream
a distance that keeps sounding.
He pulls on some music.

He was appointed to schoolhouse,
or graveyard, to hillside.
The bells dinging

and those other things friends.
They draw near,
when he speaks

it's as though an egg
spills from his mouth.
Horrifying really.

Then the egg rolls off.
He might be a cloud
or a motor,

the tall grass his father
shifts through
and the minutes

shifting like stagehands.
The service resumes.
When he opens the door

something bites him
on the cheek, like yesterday,
in moderation,

without thinking.
He pauses, then pulls
the door open again.

Acknowledgments

The author gratefully acknowledges the editors of the following publications in which these poems first appeared:

Another Chicago Magazine: "The Small Ones, in White";
A Public Space: "Have I Forgotten Anything";
Bateau Press: "under one box another," "Till It Sticks," "Some Sleep Is a Rerun";
Born Magazine: "Whereupon Lydia Sparrow";
Conduit: "Self-Portrait: Swimming in Monkeys";
Crazyhorse: "Poultry Chronicle," "Hazard Avoidance Routine";
Field: "Where I Come From," "There is a day under a box";
Forklift, Ohio: "Oafish," "When I Said I'm Changing Hats I Meant It; This Hat Is Crummy.";
The Laurel Review: "I rinsed my face and wished to be rid of it.";
Pleiades: "Right Now";
Route 9: "I Am Walking to You Now";
Verse Daily: "Poultry Chronicle," "under one box another," "Till It Sticks";
West Branch: "The Gate Snaps Open," "Night Jar." "Say Uncle."

I would like to thank the National Endowment for the Arts and The Massachusetts Cultural Council for fellowships which helped me complete this work.

Thanks also to all of those who read and encouraged these poems: Rob Casper, Lesley Hyatt, Matthew Zapruder, and especially to Michelle Markley, for everything. Thank you to Peter Conners, Sandy Knight, Melissa Hall, and Jenna Fisher. Also thanks to Alex Forman, Ezra Parzybok, and John Zarobell for their feedback and conversation.

About the Author

Michael Teig is the author of *Big Back Yard* (BOA Editions, 2003), winner of the inaugural A. Poulin, Jr. Poetry Prize. His work has appeared in many journals, including *FIELD*, *Conduit*, *Black Warrior Review*, *Bateau*, *Crazyhorse*, *Pleiades*, and *A Public Space*. He is a co-founder and editor-at-large of *jubilat*. Born in Franklin, Pennsylvania, Teig holds degrees from Oberlin College and the University of Massachusetts-Amherst. His honors include awards and fellowships from the National Endowment for the Arts, The Academy of American Poets, and the Massachusetts Cultural Council. He lives in Easthampton, Massachusetts, with his wife and son.

BOA Editions, Ltd.
American Poets Continuum Series

Colophon

BOA Editions, Ltd., a not-for-profit publisher of poetry and other literary works, fosters readership and appreciation of contemporary literature. By identifying, cultivating, and publishing both new and established poets and selecting authors of unique literary talent, BOA brings high-quality literature to the public. Support for this effort comes from the sale of its publications, grant funding, and private donations.

The publication of this book is made possible, in part, by the special support of the following individuals:

Anonymous
Kazim Ali & Marco Wilkinson
Bernadette Catalana
Anne Germanacos
Robert & Willy Hursh
X. J. & Dorothy M. Kennedy
Jack & Gail Langerak
Katy Lederer
Boo Poulin
Steven O. Russell & Phyllis Rifkin-Russell
Gerald Vorrasi